ESSENTIALS

- OF -

HOLY

LIVING

RICCARDO J. RICHBURG, SR.

ISBN: 978-1-7343100-5-4

Printed in the United States of America.

First printing, 2020.

Published by:

Shannon LeAnn Unlimited, LLC
P.O. Box 292017
Columbia, SC 29229

SLU
Shannon LeAnn
—— Unlimited ——
PUBLISHING DIVISION

DEDICATION

To my Grandma, Pastor Annette Robinson, a holy woman, that lives and teaches holiness everywhere she goes... I honor you and love you dearly.

ACKNOWLEDGMENTS

Special thanks to my wife Naomi and our children for believing in me and supporting all of my aspirations. Naomi, you make me feel like I can do anything, and you have my heart. To my mom, Joanne Davis, for keeping me in church, always being hard on me and loving me. Thank you for not letting me go. To all my aunts and uncles, especially Glenn, Yevonne, Maria, for supporting me and pushing me to be better. To my best friend Pastor Keith Smith, you are closer than a brother and have been by my side through many of life's hurts. Thanks for the wisdom and for having my back. To my editing and publishing company, Shannon LeAnn Unlimited LLC; A joy and pleasure to work with you and to have you in my corner. Thank you for helping me complete this portion of my assignment! To my Pastor and father-in-law Bishop Alfred Smalls, I have been made so much better by you. I am the father, husband, and man I am because you gave me the love of a father.

TABLE OF CONTENTS

INTRODUCTION

W e often hear statements of such, "you have to be saved, you need the Holy Ghost, and you must live right." You could probably put your examples of sayings you have heard down through the years here also. I bear record, and I am a witness that these sayings are true. But while we are being told what we should do, and what we should have, we must be instructed on how to possess it and maintain it. I am not going to say we as believers are failing in this area, because I don't feel that we are. I believe, as with all things, there is always room for improvement and growth. Knowledge is a powerful tool, and the more of it we have in a particular area, the stronger we become in that area.

The more we critique ourselves and allow ourselves to be molded, the sharper we become. The more time we spend with something, someone, or in a particular atmosphere, the more of that person, that thing, that atmosphere we take on and become. So, if we can study for school, for work, and vacation destinations, why not seek out instructions on living to obtain eternal life? As the deer pants, searches, and longs for the water brook, so must our souls want Jesus. Peter tells us that we should be as newborn babies desiring milk to be fed. We should have this same type of hunger for the word of God. The word of God will answer life's questions and pull us through some of life's most challenging moments. By taking the word in, we can grow in God. Reading and studying the word of God causes us to have a renewed mind and refreshed spirit. We become more submissive to God and the teachings of our leaders, parents, and those older than us. In this walk, we must all be accountable to someone. We must all have someone we trust and give that person the power to correct us. This is what shows if we are serious and are really striving for holiness. When we are honestly ready to commit, we are found practicing a holy lifestyle, and we welcome correction. Only through correction can we live a holy life. If we are never corrected and left to do wrong, or if we won't allow anyone the access or power to correct us, we sear our own conscience and become self-righteous. We must remember, a man is always right in his own eyes. There is also a way that seems right in those eyes of man, but the end of it is death. We don't want to perish due to the lack of knowledge or failing to receive truth through the word. We have to come to this realization; one day we will leave this life and this world. However, Our souls will live on. Every day we are making destination preparations through the life we live. Heaven or Hell? There is life after death. Yes, heaven is real, but so is hell. It's only through holy living can we move on to absolute perfection, and enter into the gates of Heaven! Let's search further.

CHAPTER 1

Holy?

Proverbs 9:10

The fear of the Lord is the beginning of wisdom: and the knowledge of the holy is understanding. KJV

B efore we can embrace something, we must understand it. We can never truly adopt or take on something without having an in-depth view of it. This way of life also can not be forced on an individual. There is such a big struggle not only in the church but in our world today. A big piece of that struggle is not understanding or knowing why we do what we do. Too long have we come to church, go to conferences, attend seminars, and webinars discussing topics that we aren't even sure we believe in. Therefore it doesn't stick or stay with us, making our life inconsistent. We find ourselves caught between two opinions and straddling the fence because we are not sure. We must know what it is we are doing, who it is we are serving, and why. So let's deal with the word Holy. Hallow, sacred; to be consecrated and dedicated to God. The word of God tells us because Jesus is holy, we should be holy. It instructs us not to conform to, go along with, agree with, or take part in things that are unholy and against God. So we must check what appears to be average or common in the world against Christ's instructions. To be Holy means to be set apart from uncleanliness, dedicated to God, clean, pure. So there must be a separation, a difference if you will, between what is holy and unholy, clean and unclean, pure and impure. If you see where a difference isn't but should be, you put it there. To be like Jesus means to be holy. Plainly, those that are holy should be different from those who are not. When we are holy, we have an intimate relationship with God. We present our bodies, our minds, our hearts to him for his use. We no longer practice sin, or willingly, premeditatedly take part in sin. Our lives are solely and wholly dedicated to God. This requires us to give up our love for the things of this world. Because what you love, you will cherish, and what you cherish will have a form of power and control over you. If it hurts, you hurt. If it's angry, you're angry. If it doesn't fit into what is righteous and holy in the eyes of God, then you don't fit. When we are living holy, it's evident. We don't have to hold up a poster board, but it's easily seen. The way we walk, talk, dress, live, the places we go, and the company we keep. When we are really holy, we don't do things that are offensive to God or get upset when those things are brought to our attention.

For this reason, we must be rooted and grounded in the word. The world pulls at holiness every day and shouts, "It doesn't take all that." We must not be so easily deceived. We must lay aside every weight and sin that can and will beset us if we are not vigilant. We must run this race with patience. Sometimes when we start wide open on something, we crash halfway through due to exhaustion or lack of resources. But when we start at a moderate low pace, break for a while, plan, then come back moving a little faster, we tend to cover more ground. Often, it is more beneficial to move in smaller intervals. We find out that we have made it further by taking our time. That's how Satan does. He doesn't try to take us down all at once, but little by little. The small foxes spoil the vine. After a while, we will turn to look back and try to figure out, "How did I get so far away from holiness?" Holiness is not a religion or a denomination, but a lifestyle, or way of life. Living this way changes your entire outlook on life. This way changes your very perception and thought process concerning everything. When we walk this way, we present our bodies as a living sacrifice holy and acceptable unto God! So holiness becomes what we need, what we want, and who we are. Then and only then, we become more and more dedicated to Jesus, the holy one we love. "Follow peace with all men and holiness without which, no man shall see the Lord!" We need the Holy Ghost, the spirit of God, our comforter, and keeper.

"When we are holy, we have received Christ, we live according to the word, attend to the things of Christ, and we are Christ-like. Now, let's ask ourselves, are we Holy?"

Bishop Alfred Smalls

CHAPTER 2

Be Sure

Joshua 25:15

And if it seem evil unto you to serve the LORD, choose ye this day whom ye will serve; whether the gods which your fathers served that were on the other side of the flood, or the gods of the Amorites, in whose land ye dwell: but as for me and my house, we will serve the Lord. KJV

My grandmother, who is the matriarch of our family, and my mom kept us in church. We went to multiple services on Sunday, rehearsals, meetings, cleaning, and bible study during the week. It was nothing to be at the church every day of the week. My grandmother led us to Christ and kept her hand in our backs. Even when we didn't want to go, we had no choice in the matter. We always heard, "as for me and my house, we will serve the Lord." She took us until I fell in love with Jesus and always wanted to go to church for myself. At this point, it was no longer just what she wanted, but what I desired. I remember getting saved. I remember the week-long revival and how powerful the service was. No one threatened me, and no one dragged me to the altar, no one used reverse psychology on me. The preacher just stood and preached about heaven and hell. She told us about paradise and how great heaven will be. We felt that we had something to look forward to. She also talked about the destination of hell and how awful it would be. She mentioned that both destinations are eternal resting places, and there was no coming back. Also, there was nothing we or anyone could do to change our destination once we die. But she said every day God wakes us up, we have another chance, and we have an opportunity right now. I remember feeling Jesus tugging at my heart and hearing his voice say come. I walked to the altar and gave God my life that night. Having been in the church since a baby, I knew right from wrong. I sat in service after service, heard prayer after prayer, and taught in bible study after bible study. But I had to get to a point where I made a decision. It had to be my choice. I heard Jesus in that revival, and I didn't harden my heart. I opened it up and let him in. Even if you were not raised in the church, you will still be presented with the opportunity to get to know Jesus in a better way. It may very well be while you are reading this book. At some point, you will feel and hear him calling you. When you hear God, when you feel the spirit move on you, succumb to it. Let Jesus have his way in you. I haven't been perfect or always done right, but I made a conscious decision that night to seek Jesus for the rest of my life. I was as sure then as I am now, and I had to make the decision. You can't be forced or scared into Jesus, and if you are, you won't keep him. There is also no need to fake this life if you don't want it. That is dangerous, and God is not mocked. For this faith, healing, deliverance, and Jesus' lifestyle to work, we must be sure. We must be sincere and convinced in our decision to walk this way. Holiness is a choice, and it must be chosen by each individual freely and personally if it's what they want. Whatever you do, be sure that this is what you want. God is not a toy, a plaything, or something to do in your spare time. He is not just a resource place to run to for help when you are in trouble.

God is bigger than that. He wants all of us, totally dedicated to him, at all times. Often we get tied up in what momma wants or what daddy wants. We even get overwhelmed by what our spouses want and what our children desire. We may feel pressured by what the preacher stands and declares. All of this happens because we hear and feel the truth in what they are saying or asking. Whether it's right or wrong, it resonates within us. We're being moved because of those we love and want to please. I ask you today, how long will you not move as Christ knocks at the door? How long will you wait before you make up in your mind who you will serve? It's time to make a decision. *What's it going to be? When will you answer? How Long will it take you to make up your mind?*

"*I gave the Lord my whole life, and I won't ever go back!*"

Pastor Annette Robinson

CHAPTER 3

Waking Up & Day to Day Living With Jesus

———————◗◦◖———————

Romans 12:2

And be not conformed to this world: but be he transformed by the renewing of your mind, that ye may prove what is that good, and acceptable, and perfect, will of God. KJV

Questions that came to mind after that revival as a new convert, and questions that I get asked to this day by others that are searching: Can I do this saved thing? Can I really live this life? Is this gonna be too hard? Can I still have fun? How do I keep this that I have found? After I gave Jesus my life, I was surrounded, or rather I surrounded myself with those of like mind. I hung around those that I saw live this life, and I inquired of them how to do this. The process of sanctification involves us turning from our unjust and evil ways, and begin to seek out that which is right in the sight of God. As our knowledge of good and evil increases, our life should change. As we sanctify ourselves, crucify this flesh, and practice a righteous lifestyle, the God of peace will sanctify us wholly. One of the first things I learned is while

7

we are not perfect; we should be seeking perfection. Still, we must remember, every day that Jesus wakes us up, it's another chance we have to get it right, and another day he gave us to live and witness for him. That doesn't mean do things that are wrong and ask for forgiveness just because the grace is there. Don't give yourself a crutch saying no one's perfect, or take the scripture out of context, "We all have sinned and come short of the glory of God." One thing this flesh will do is try to justify itself when we know that we are wrong. Consider this, there is no good thing in this flesh, and when we want to do right, evil is always present. So the opportunity and encouragement to do wrong are just as present as the voice speaking to you to do right. This is why we must train ourselves and build a healthy relationship with God. This starts when we wake up every morning. We should start every day with prayer and meditation. I know some say, I have to get up early to go to work. I understand that, but set your alarm 20-30 minutes early, and give God that time. We get up earlier to go out of town, or go shopping. We make adjustments to get overtime and do everything else we want to do when we want to do it. Let's put God in that same category. Then take it further by praying at different times throughout the day.

Prayer is our communication with God. Our conversation with him is so imperative to keep a relationship with him healthy. Also, take time daily to read and study the word of God. By doing so, we learn more about him and grow stronger in him. It's good to hear sermons, hear teachings, be in worship services, and yes, all of that is a must and has its place. When you know for yourself, it changes the dynamic of the relationship. When you know for yourself, no one can take it from you. When you know for yourself, it enhances the worship experience you attend and opens understanding in the sermons and teachings you hear.

We must also set aside times to fast before the Lord. Remember, Jesus told the disciples when they were trying to cast out a spirit, this kind goeth not out but by fasting and prayer. Maybe set aside a few days out of the month or one day a week. When you fast or turn your plate down, you deny the fleshly man and build the spirit man. During this time, your interactions with the public are minimal, your consumption of food and other regular things (tv, social media, shopping, phone conversation, etc.) is minimal to none. During this time, you want to shut away if you can. Pray, study, read, meditate, and get in the presence of God. This is for those that are serious about getting strong and staying strong in God. We must have a daily, holy lifestyle. To possess the power and command the authority, we have to spend time with God. The true miracles and the real signs and wonders happen because someone was praying and fasting. The signs follow us when someone has been spending time with Jesus. When you are in the presence of the savior, after you come out, people know it. You can't be before Jesus, and your confidence not be lifted. You don't bask in his presence, and your faith does not increase. No, my brother, my sister, when you have been with the redeemer, you come out singing a new song. You emerge speaking a new language, and things around you begin to manifest. Why, because we were in his presence and the residue of his presence doesn't go away when you leave his presence. Walking with him daily keeps us in the right posture.

"I can't be like everybody, because then I can't draw anybody! I got to be like Jesus to make a difference!"

Evangelist Naomi Richburg

CHAPTER 4

Your Inner Circle

1 Corinthians 15:33

Be not deceived: evil communications corrupt good manners. KJV

A challenging topic for some. It will show where you are in your walk and pursuit of God. At this juncture, we also see our maturity as Christians. Just as the people in your inner circle can help you, they can most certainly hinder you. I know it's difficult to put up borders and sever year-long ties from family and friends. But we have to know if they are not going in the direction we are going, they can hinder our efforts. If they are not helping the cause, they are hurting the cause. In the spiritual realm, there are no middle ground or gray areas. It is only good and evil. You're either with me or against me. Before you disagree, how many times have you found yourself doing something wrong that your friends encouraged? How many times have you felt convicted or condemned because of places you've gone, conversations you've entertained, or the company you've kept? How many things have you said, watched, or listened to, and you just felt terrible because you knew it was wrong or felt a conflict within yourself? But your friends, who know you are a believer, know your stance as a Christian and know that you are not like them, drive you to these places. They leave laughing, but you leave broken and hurt, and before long, you don't feel God like you used to. What about the same friends that lead you out there, turn around and mock you, "I thought you were saved," "and you supposed to be a Christian," "see you ain't supposed to be doing stuff like me." See, they may like you, but they don't respect you. The same people that egg you on will put an egg on your face. Somewhere along the line, if you're not careful, you will lose yourself and your posture. You go to shake yourself like Sampson, and your strength doesn't come. You go to call Jesus, and you can't hear his voice or feel his presence like you once did. Like I mentioned in chapter 1, you wonder how you get so far away. When did it happen, where did I go wrong, and how did I let this happen? Guard your heart. Hide the word of the lord there that you might not sin against him. Check your circle now. You still love them and pray for them, but limit your exposure to them. The proper exposure can be life-changing, career-advancing, reach increasing, and name echoed for the better. However, the wrong exposure can change you, cripple your voice, credibility, trustworthiness, and your ability to sustain yourself or anyone around you. Be honest with your circle, and more importantly, be honest with yourself. If you're not drawing them and they are not changing, then you are. Yes, you are. No really, yes, you are changing. If you find yourself here and can be honest, you will admit I lost some ground dealing with some of these people, in some of my circles. Healing that I once had, has receded. The place in me that used to trust God was replaced with fear. The voice that used to speak life now speaks death and destruction, WHAT HAPPENED! You let them draw you, and you changed. But come on back to who you are. You are not like them. Two can't walk together, except they agree. Do you agree with your circle and their lifestyle? You know the truth, and you know what's right. So don't override what you know to be true, for a friend. Your soul's eternal resting place just may be at stake. Overlooking principles and practices like these now only set you up for a more significant pitfall, flawed character, and discredited witness later.

"Be careful who you let in, and who you call 'friend'. The devil will hook you up with people that try to teach you the tricks and trades of holiness."

Bishop Alfred Smalls

CHAPTER 5

Be A Witness

Acts 1:8

But ye shall receive power, after that the Holy Ghost is come upon you: and ye shall be witnesses unto me both in Jerusalem, and in all Judaea, and in Samaria, and unto the uttermost part of the earth.

Our first instruction or call is to be a witness of Jesus Christ. This is also an essential part of living a holy life. We should not, we cannot obtain all of this knowledge and experience, and then keep it to ourselves. This is the critical piece of a holy life, being a witness for Jesus. When you walk this way truly, you can't keep it to yourself. You feel a burden and a passion for winning souls. You will want others to be as you are and accept Jesus as their personal savior. Our previous chapter spoke of your circle. Your circle can also kill your witness. It may not be right, but people will pass judgment on you according to your circle. You don't want your good evil spoken of, but can you blame them? How many times have you, I or anybody said, (and be honest) "Oh, they can't preach to me"? They can't tell me anything. I can't believe they still have him/her up operating. Why are they still preaching, singing, serving, etc.? It's because of their lifestyle, who they hang around, the things they say, and the things they do. We are not passing judgment, but we can tell the tree by the fruit it bears. I'm not talking about gossip or church rumors, but what we have seen and discerned for ourselves. This is another area where we must be truthful. We have to stop propping people up as something they are not. If the truth is being told, it's not judging, its just the truth. There is a difference in covering someone and covering up for someone. When we prop up, support, and endorse sin, it causes us, the church to lose our witness. To be honest, before we can witness, influence, or lead anybody, they want to SEE an example. They want to see us practicing what we preach. They want to know if you walk what you talk about. In clarity, they want to know if the place they are receiving truth from is indeed true. They want to know if the source of their knowledge is proven and sincere. Some are looking to make sure you are different from them. They may never say it or tell you, but they are hoping every day that you stay truthful and hold on. You got to love God and people to do this wholeheartedly. You must have patience and be not so easily discouraged. This takes time, it's not convenient, nor is it cheap. This is where true believers show up. This is how we know who is true of God, those that display love for one another. With love and kindness have I drawn thee, the bible declares, but that doesn't mean cover up sin. That doesn't mean give wrongdoing a pass. It means to know how to talk to someone knowing we all were once where they are, IN SIN. We are our brother's and sister's keeper, and it's our duty to pull their feet out of the fire. Don't give up on them. God didn't give up on you. When you have done all you can, just pray for them. You don't have to constantly wear them out with the word, or jump on them every time you see them. He who wins souls is wise. Pray and discern before you go in on someone. Stand up in your family, on your job, in your day to day activities. Don't be afraid to walk through the doors that God opens. Someone's life is on the line.

Remember, every soul is too precious to lose. Someone witnessed to you believer, and someone witnessed to me. I am so glad they did! Think about it, aren't you glad that you decided to make Jesus your choice? Don't you think they will be too? Don't you think they will feel like you feel about Jesus when they get what you have? We fill so much of our day talking about vain imaginations, and sometimes useless, unchangeable things, not realizing someone out there on your job, in your family, at the gas station, in the grocery store is depending on you to give them the bread of life. Where is your witness? Lift up your voice in the land. Cry loud the ways and words of the Lord. Don't hide out, and don't conform. Someone's life is depending on your witness.

"It's our duty to tell everyone about Jesus and salvation. If the believers keep quiet, how else will they know?"

Pastor Annette Robinson

CHAPTER 6

Ultimate Goal

---

1 Thessalonians 4:16-17

For the Lord himself shall descend from heaven with a shout, with the voice of the archangel, and with the trump of God: And the dead in Christ shall rise first: then we which are alive and remain shall be caught up together with him in the clouds, to meet the Lord in the air: and so shall we ever be with the Lord. KJV

We started in the introduction talking about heaven, and we will close on it too. What does it profit a man to gain the whole world and lose his soul? I want us all to prosper in this world as God does, in health and wealth. But to win it all, AND still, die, and go to hell? The eternal darkness and eternal suffering? Please don't get me wrong. You can be saved and live an exciting, balanced, and fulfilling life too! This is an area that is not highlighted enough. We can laugh and let our hair down. Take your shoes off, relax, and put your feet up. Enjoy the extended family and friends. Take the trips out of town, sightsee, shop, and enjoy your life here on earth. Catch a flight out to a place of interest or take a cruise out on God's blue sea. God made it for us to enjoy here.

Just don't throw your holy principles and morals out the window when you do. Don't bypass everything we just covered in these few chapters, for a few moments of sinful pleasure. This is why we were shackled by so many rules and regulations in the early church. We lacked self-control and discipline. So in an attempt to help us keep ourselves and save our lives, we were just told not to partake in certain things because it was a sin. Some things were not sinning, but because of the lack of self-control, these worldly things led many to sin. The intentions of many leaders are honest and admirable to help you stay saved and help you want to stay saved.

However, as we covered in chapter two, you must be sure for yourself and want this for yourself. Understand me, we don't have to sin to have a good time. We don't have to defile our temple to have a good time. We don't have to crucify Jesus again to have a good time. We don't have to throw away a holy lifestyle to live day to day on this earth. Don't look at a Holy lifestyle with tunnel vision, and don't look at it through the eyes of the world either. Live as long as you can, but don't forget that one day we have to leave here. Live right so you can die right. This is not meant or intended to bring fear, but we have to start the conversations back up about heaven and hell! Because believe it or not, when we die, our soul will go to one or the other. There is indeed life after death. There is hope beyond the grave. Jesus proved it when he rolled back the stone. There is still hope for us today! All we have to do is come, and let God do the work, let him break us and make us over. Let him save us and fill us with the Holy Ghost. Let him burn away everything, not like him, and set our souls ablaze with fire from glory. Stand in His way every day, where he has to touch us as He passes by. If you call Him, He will come. Yes, He will answer His name, and yes, He will answer by fire.

Jesus is near to the brokenhearted and saves the one of a contrite spirit. Let him make us new. For the scriptures declare if any man be in Christ, he is a new creature, for all old things are passed away and behold all things are new. Let Jesus make you whole today. Come clean with Him, He already knows anyway. We are truly living to live again. Deliverance is here, freedom is here, healing is here, love is here, hope is here, joy is here, and peace is here. Just know whatever it is we need to fill the void in our lives, and the hole in our souls is here, at the altar. We don't have to keep going in the same cycles. Jesus wants to make us whole today. His right hand is extended, better yet, he stands all day long with his arms outstretched saying come to me. We can do this, yes you reading this right now, can do this. We can be saved, sanctified, holy ghost filled, and live this Holy life. We have been granted access to the essentials of a Holy life. Don't let this moment pass you by and not accept the Savior. He came for you. You can go to your local assembly or make an altar right there where you are now, but COME, COME, COME TO JESUS!

"When I close my eyes on this side, the next face I see will be Jesus's face. I got something to look forward to."

Bishop Alfred Smalls

19

Elder Riccardo J. Richburg Sr.

Riccardo Richburg was born in Sumter, SC to a proud family. Riccardo grew up in Sumter, SC, and graduated from Sumter High School, and he was accepted to Greenville University. He was so academically passionate that he did not have to pay anything for his education, but based on his upbringing, he continued to work to help his mother! He received his certification in Computer Technology, Networking, and Programming.

Upon his birth, he was welcomed by his loving mother, who believed that the best place for her only son was in the house of the Lord. Riccardo came to know the Lord through the ministry of his grandmother, Pastor Annette Robinson, who he credits with leading him to Christ, and never letting him get by with anything! For many years he was proud to be a member of New Jerusalem Fire-Baptized Holiness Church in Sumter SC in the renowned Columbia District. He served on the Sunday School Teacher's staff, Minister's Staff, Pastor's Anniversary Committee, and he was a musician. He was a very great asset to his pastors during this time.

In 2005, Riccardo began working in Florence, SC which is where he met the woman that he would later ask to become his wife. After a brief courtship, he asked her father for permission to ask for her hand in marriage. In March of 2007, Riccardo Richburg married the former Naomi Smalls in holy matrimony. They have three children, Rhagin Julia Richburg, Racquel Jo'Di Richburg, and Riccardo Jaquar Richburg Jr.

By the end of 2008, Riccardo had joined The Inner Court Apostolic Church, and together, this husband and wife duo work tirelessly to support their church, The Inner Court Apostolic Church in Jesus Christ in Florence, SC. Under the leadership of Bishop A. Smalls, Elder Richburg is flourishing in the Gospel and many other areas of the ministry! He is a very active member and can be found helping each auxiliary in several leadership roles. He serves as the Finance Chairman, Youth President, Sunday School Teacher, and also the keyboard/organist as well as a drummer!

Elder Richburg is known to be a faithful man who loves his family and the Lord Jesus! His motto is, These signs shall follow those that believe! There is no turning back and no stopping for him in this gospel way. For the rest of his life, he declares he will be serving God and continue to let his life be a witness to bring lost souls to Christ.

CONTACT THE AUTHOR

For Booking Engagements, Book Tours, Conference, and more:

Elder Riccardo J. Richburg Sr.
Email: riccardorichburg@yahoo.com
Facebook: Riccardo Richburg

www.ingramcontent.com/pod-product-compliance
Lightning Source LLC
Chambersburg PA
CBHW031936080426
42734CB00007B/712